PETER ILYICH TCHAIK...

MARCHE SLAVE
SLAVONIC MARCH
SLAWISCHER MARSCH

for Orchestra
Op. 31

Ernst Eulenburg Ltd

London · Mainz · Madrid · New York · Paris · Prague · Tokyo · Toronto · Zürich

MARCHE SLAVE

Peter I. Tchaikovsky
(1840–1893)
Op.31

Moderato in modo di marcia funebre

2

12

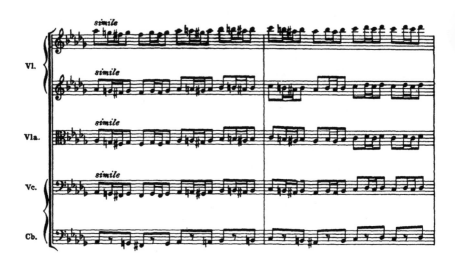

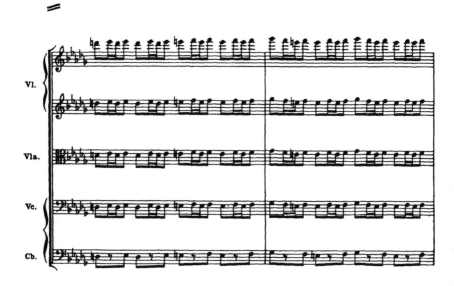

E.E.4412

28

E. E. 4412

E. E. 4412

E.E.4412

38

E. E. 4413

E. E. 4412

150

E. E. 4412

E. E. 4412

Più mosso. Allegro

Andante molto maestoso

Allegro risoluto

E. E. 4412

240